D0272133

TERRIBLE PETS

Compiled by

SARAH KENNEDY

BBC BOOKS

Sarah Kennedy, a former speech and drama teacher, made the move into television and radio in 1973. Her wide experience ranges from the Saturday night hit show *Game for a Laugh* to programmes covering the arts, current affairs and travel; and from the wedding of the Duke and Duchess of York to the twenty-four hour British Telethon. She is currently working with Dr Desmond Morris on the *Animal Country* television series, which is now in its eighth year, and on *Speaking Volumes* and *Thicker Than Water* for BBC Radio 2. Her awards include *Female Personality of the Year* for ITV in 1982 and for the BBC in 1984; *TV Woman of the Year*, awarded by the Variety Club of Great Britain in 1984; and the 1995 *Sony Breakfast Show Award* for *Dawn Patrol*, her programme on BBC Radio 2.

Sarah Kennedy loves gardening, Shakespeare and cooking. Humour is a very important ingredient in her life and work, and the two editions of her bestselling and brilliantly funny book *The Terrible Twos* raised a large amount of money for the BBC's *Children in Need*.

Special thanks are due to:

Sarah Kennedy's BBC Radio 2 *Dawn Patrol* programme who have given permission for their
letters and poems to be included in this book,
Christine Gordon-Jones of Cobra & Bellamy
for allowing us to use her puppies and cat, Burma, for the cover,
Heather Cary, for her cartoons
and David Ward for taking the cover photographs.

Published by BBC Worldwide Limited,
Woodlands, 80 Wood Lane, London W12 OTT.
First published 1996.
ISBN 0 563 38727 0

Stories © individual contributors, 1996
Compilation © Sarah Kennedy

Set in Adobe Garamond
Printed in Great Britain by Martins of Berwick Ltd
Bound in Great Britain by Hunter and Foulis Ltd, Edinburgh
Cover printed by Lawrence Allen Ltd, Weston-super-Mare

**A royalty of 4 per cent of the retail price of this book will be paid
to the PDSA (People's Dispensary for Sick Animals) on every copy sold**

Barbara Nash (Project Editor, BBC Worldwide Ltd) has made every effort to contact the
contributors to this book. Should she have failed to do so, she will be pleased to correct this,
after notification, at the earliest possible opportunity.

P R E F A C E

Dawn patrollers are well known in BBC Radio 2 for writing simply brilliant letters. I throw out a talking point, and you lot are off like greyhounds after the rabbit. This reminds me of the *The Terrible Twos* tale: toddler watching dog-racing on TV rushes into the kitchen – 'Mum, some doggies on TV were chasing a rabbit and the rabbit won'.

After the amazing success of *The Terrible Twos* raising a large amount of money for BBC Children In Need, I never planned a second book. It just happened; and, once again, it's OUR book. A listener wrote: 'YOU couldn't have done it without US and we couldn't have done it without YOU'.

This book, then, is a small thank-you for all the enormous pleasure, company, fun and love our pets give us.

Why *Terrible Pets*? It all started with my aged Ps. My mother, the Beatific Mary, left on top of the fridge a tranqillizer wedged in a piece of Cheddar. This was for McGregor, a yellow Labrador pup, who hated cars. The vet prescribed the pills, Mother produced the cheese, Father – hungry for his lunch – picked up the morsel and the rest is family history. McGregor bounced and woofed up and down on the back seat; Father, with nice wet nose, started to fall asleep at the wheel!

As soon as I told this tale on *Dawn Patrol*, the mail flood-gates opened. In poured hilarious tales of terrible pets.

I was then introduced to Heather Cary. She's done our cartoons; and Barbara Nash has again put her editorial stamp on *Terrible Pets*, just as she did on *The Terrible Twos*. In fact, the monster on my lap is Barbara's pup, Bertie – the naughtiest of the litter!

I do hope you enjoy *Terrible Pets*. What shall we do next?

Sarah Kennedy

WOOFS

Dear Sarah,

Please please help me. I'm writing to you because I know you are kind to dumb animals. My name is Barney Murphy. I am a rather large six-year-old Dalmatian and I live with my family, Rona, Tony and their two daughters Helen and Susan.

Helen is getting married to Martin Willoughby and, as you can imagine, everybody is very excited and looking forward to the Big Day. However, I heard them talking, when they thought I was asleep, and, shock of shocks, I am not being invited. There is some pathetic excuse that I get excited, jump up at people, sometimes knock them over, lick their faces and ears etc., etc.

I don't understand – when will they realize that getting excited, jumping up, licking people's faces and ears is what I do. I'm a dog for goodness sake, not a brain surgeon – one despairs of humans sometimes! Anyhow, as a result I am being sent to kennels for a few days. I expect they will tell me I am going on holiday, which is what they usually say. This means I will not be here on the Big Day and I am really disappointed. I was so looking forward to seeing all the family, posing for the photographs and generally making a nuisance of myself, but it's not to be.

The worst thing is that I won't be there to give Helen and Martin my love and best wishes.

I was at a complete loss until I thought of you. I know you love animals from watching you on TV's Animal Country *with Mr Desmond Morris and listening to you each morning on the radio with all your funny stories, especially the ones about dogs.*

So I am writing to ask you if you would please be kind enough to let people know how dogs feel about these things, and if you can also wish Helen and Martin all the best on the Big Day.

I will be ever so grateful and, if we meet some day, I promise not to knock you over but I will probably lick your ears.

Barney Murphy

A mere trifle

I had lovingly prepared a sponge in a bowl for a trifle, put in the sherry and left it to soak in while I went out. On arrival home, I noticed Precious, my cat, looked cross-eyed and groggy. With the exception of a few crumbs, she had eaten the whole sponge.

Julie Rochefort

Tea for one more?

Janet and Bob were expecting friends for tea. In mid-afternoon they arrived, along with Boxer dog. Houseproud Janet thought bringing the dog along was a bit of a cheek, and did not relish the thought of dog-hair all over her carpet, but she politely gritted her teeth and held her tongue even when the dog jumped up on the settee and slobbered for titbits. When dinner was served the dog followed, insisting on visiting everybody in turn for scraps from the table, then settled back on the settee again while coffee was served.

'You certainly spoil your dog,' one of the friends said suddenly to Janet.

'My dog!' Janet replied, nearly choking. 'You mean, your dog.'

'No,' said the friend astonished, 'it arrived on the doorstep the same time as us.'

Exit Boxer followed by some unrepeatable words!

Maggie Foord

Toy boy

My four-year-old granddaughter was heart-broken at the death of the first dog she had ever loved. We both cried together and then talked it through in-depth with me struggling to come up with the appropriate answers to her life-and-death questions. She finally dried her tears, thought for a moment, then said matter-of-factly: 'Can we stuff his body, so I can have him as a toy?'

She had obviously just remembered a museum visit.

Barbara Clarke

Return to sender

Like most Labradors, my parents' golden Labrador, Boo, loved help-ing by carrying things around, anything from eggs from the hen-house, to an innocent passer-by's gloves. Boo could teach Fagin a thing or two about pick-pocketing.

Anyway, living in the country, as my parents do, it was about a mile to the nearest postbox, and, having an important letter which needed to be posted, my dad, then in his seventies, set out with Boo to post the letter.

At the letter box the postman was just getting into his van having emptied the box. He rolled down his window to take the letter from my dad.

Before either man knew what was happening Boo had taken the letter from the postman's hand, and was gaily trotting off towards home, tail wagging wildly. (Collecting the post in the morning at the gate was a recently acquired party trick.) Naturally she ignored all calls to stop, or anything else my dad could think of to shout at her. Why is it dogs get a convenient deafness when they want to?

Anyway, when he eventually arrived home, Dad found a tri-umphant beaming Boo waiting on the doorstep, soggy letter still in her mouth. How could anyone be cross with such a helpful friend! The letter somehow lost its importance and waited until the next day when it had dried out.

Judith Twyman

Sock-it-to-them, Emma

Emma, our dotty Dobermann bitch, was born a glutton, able to swallow anything in micro-seconds. One of her more revolting 'fancies' – she was obviously still hungry after her breakfast – emerged when we were walking along a grassy cliff edge by a beach at Lee-on-Solent. Despite all our cries, she constantly rushed off, zig-zagging her fat ungainly body up and down the crowded beach where people lay, bodies stripped off, by their bundles of clothes.

Soon, from the sudden activity of the sun-bathers and swimmers, it became clear that she was grabbing guarded and unguarded bundles of clothing, tossing them about, making her selection and running off. By the time she reached us, hotly pursued by several irate men, she looked even more swollen than usual, but only had one item trailing from her mouth.

We were not, however, left in the dark for long – she had visited each bundle in turn and cleared the beach of dirty socks. Needless to say, while we dealt with the rumpus from the ex-sock-owners, she swallowed the evidence and beat a rapid retreat.

Ian C. Roberts

Requiem for innocence

I wrote the following poem when I had to have my first Sheep Dog put down – a horrid expression – when she was sixteen years old. She was given to me as a pup – as a welcoming present from a neighbouring farmer – when I moved to Devon from Birmingham to start farming. So, we both learned 'how' together and this added poignancy when I lost her.

The poem is taken from my first book, *Requiem for Innocence*, and I had a lot of phone calls from people who were 'touched' by it, including one from a person who was: 'Pleasantly surprised that a farmer could write such a sympathetic poem about an animal'!

Sheep Dog passing

He said, 'You needn't wait
if you'd rather' and called the nurse.
'It's for the best,' He said.

Whose best I'd like to know. It's
all very well for Him,
all glass and stainless steel.
'It will be quick,' He said
and filled the syringe.
'There will be no pain,' He said
and clipped the hair above the vein.

Holding her, she licked my hand and
understood: anything would be a piece of cake
after nights of blizzards on the moors
to pinpoint buried sheep, and rescue lambs
or, to a whistle, in the noontide heat
outrun, collect and fetch far flocks
from hills to lusher grounds.
Her eyes reminded me of little things, shared
times to treasure garnered over half a life.

'It's done,' He said
and dropped the needle in the stainless bowl.
At peace she watched me, sighed and slept.

Him in his glass and stainless world
said there would be no pain;
but he was wrong.

R. A. Chesterfield

Is there a lobster in the house?

We had invited ten good friends for a lobster supper. In the morning my husband collected twelve lobsters which I arranged beautifully on beds of mustard-and-cress on two basket trays. With the salad pre-prepared, all I had to do was to cook a few potatoes when our guests arrived. After a few pre-supper drinks I took off to the kitchen and was aghast to be greeted by bits of mustard-and-cress all over the floor. Heart beating faster than ever before, I then took in that only two of the lobsters were left on the tray and that five yellow Labradors were now sleeping soundly. They had eaten the other ten lobsters, including shells, whiskers – everything but the mustard-and-cress.

'Don't panic,' my husband, John, said, when I coaxed him into the kitchen and panic-strickenly told him the score. 'Keep them all drinking while I drive back to the lobster restaurant and buy ten more.'

One hour later, he returned triumphantly and, at the strawberries-and-cream stage, we entertained our completely 'blotto' guests with the lobster-happy Labradors' story. It was the most expensive supper party we ever gave – and doubtless the best meal the dogs ever had!

Nancy Dove

What a good boy, am I!

Mick, our dog, it has to be said, is a naughty but obedient dog. He persists in investigating the contents of carrier bags when I arrive home from the supermarket, but obligingly responds to my commands. Hearing him at it, while I was trafficking carrier-bags to and from the car, I shouted: 'Drop it'.

He did at once to do him justice. It was a box of eggs! And, to add insult to injury, he trod and slithered all through the mess, as he came, tail down, to say sorry he had been caught with egg on his face.

Vicky Arscott

What's in a name?

I was walking up the High Street when I noticed a stolid-looking infant dressed in a pixie hat and chunky coat waiting in his buggy. Tethered to the pushchair was a puppy, which began to wag all over as I approached.

'What's his name?' I asked the child.

'Bloody bugger,' came the dead-pan reply.

Christine Hart

No parking

Returning to the car park I saw, with a sinking heart, yet another traffic warden snapping her book shut and sticking a ticket to the windscreen of my car. Baffled and bewildered, I stood peering at the spot where I knew I had stuck the parking ticket. After a moment, angry with myself and none the wiser, convinced by now I was going bonkers, my eyes strayed from the windscreen to our Cocker Spaniel, Teddy, sitting on the front seat. Bored with waiting, he had taken the ticket and reparked it in his tummy.

I decided to pay the fine without even trying to explain.

Bobbin Eaglen

Follow that deckchair

On holiday in Cornwall, we had to tether Herbie, our Yorkshire Terrier, to a deckchair because he kept pinching the ball my husband and the boys were trying to play with. After watching their antics for a while, I decided to go for a paddle. So I piled the picnic things on to the deckchair and set off. I had just reached the water when there was a shout from the boys. I turned and there was Herbie towing the laden deckchair behind him determined at all costs not to be left behind. He looked like one of the contestants from the 'strongest man in the world'!

Hilary Nash

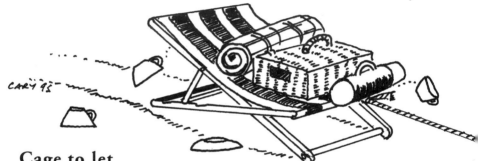

Cage to let

Our Irish Setter, Darrig, adored all small mammals, such as hamsters, guinea pigs etc., (as have all my Setters), and used to gaze longingly at the guinea pig in her raised cage.

One day I returned home to find the guinea pig scuttling round our courtyard and was amazed to see that Darrig had opened the cage and had managed to squeeze inside, even squeezing himself through the small opening into the sleeping area. The whole cage was bursting with Setter. He was dozing happily and we had to dismantle the cage to get him out.

Beryl Neighbour

Sex pest!

A few years ago we had a lovely Boxer, Nikki. One day as I was walking him along the promenade, he vanished into the long grass on Lovers' Hill.

I thought he was chasing rabbits until I heard screams and shouts! Soon, Nikki appeared, grinning all over his face with a bra dangling from his teeth. He was so pleased with himself, wagging his little stump of a tail and dancing back and forth, the bra swinging. I made several desperate grabs at it, but he thought it would be great fun to play tug-of-war.

Meanwhile, the disgruntled lovers were leaping around in the long grass, furious at having their passion interrupted, and the lady miffed at having her undies filched.

Nikki absolutely refused to relinquish his prize trophy and walked all the way home with it dangling from his jaws. He was delighted, whether with the bra, or the consternation he had caused, I was never quite sure.

Roxy Thompson

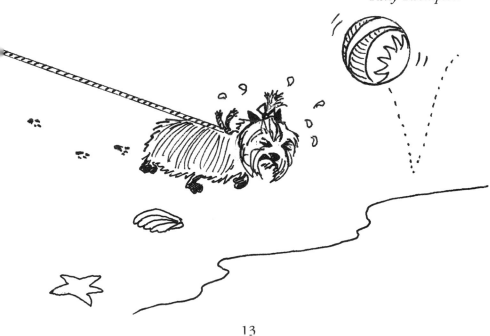

Feeling sheepish

It was a crisp sunny winter's day and my daughter and I set out to walk our three Golden Retrievers Bonnie, Pickle and Pepper on a nearby beach. It was a bit of a treat for them and excitement was at fever pitch. As I opened the hatchback, out they all bounded, up and over the dunes, heading for the beach.

My daughter and I followed at a more leisurely pace, expecting to find all three dogs waiting for us on the beach. Sure enough, Bonnie and Pepper ran up to us, but Pickle was nowhere to be seen. We called and called but there was no sign of her. Thinking she may have returned to the car we anxiously retraced our steps over the dunes and looked towards the car park. There we beheld an absolutely incredible scenario.

Near a parked car, in a circle, sat a white Poodle, a white Westie, two yellow Labradors, a strange Retriever and our Pickle. All were completely under the spell of an old Border Collie. The Collie's owner apologized profusely, explaining that her dog imagined all pale coloured dogs were sheep and insisted on rounding them up and herding them!

Hilary Searle

Just testing

I had four G.S.Ds – three dogs and one bitch – and we had a purpose-designed dog-proof garden with a very secure wooden fence. One evening, however, there was a knock on the door. On opening it, I was confronted by my next-door neighbours' very irate daughter who informed me that her mother had been bitten by one of my dogs, and had just returned from hospital where she had received treatment. I really could not understand how she had been bitten as the garden was totally enclosed and dog-proof. So, I did no more, but flew round to my neighbours' house in a right old state, fearing the worst. On arrival, I was ushered into the front room where my neighbour, Molly, a very sweet Irish lady, was sitting nursing a finger with a very large bandage on it. She was a bit tearful, and I could not apologize enough for what had happened.

'Molly' I said, 'please tell me, how did the dog bite your finger?'

'Well,' she said in her soft Irish brogue, 'I put my finger through one of those little knotholes in the fence, waggled it a bit just to see what would happen, and someone bit me.'

To this day, I do not know how I kept a straight face! On return home, I went into the garden and proceeded to block up every small dog-height knothole in the fence. Which dog had bitten her, we never did know, but sometimes my sweet Misty used to stare rather wistfully at that fence, wondering, perhaps, if that sausage was going to appear again!

Ros Moore

Murphy's law

We lived in a house that backed on to a major park and Murphy, our Irish Wolf Hound, because of his size and weight (fifteen-and-a-half stone!) used to take himself for a walk every day by simply walking straight through a large thorn hedge.

One day we were walking with him near some lakes, at the end of which was a small, high, narrow ice-cream caravan. Murphy suddenly ran ahead, skidded to a halt, sat down, and the ice-cream vendor unwrapped an ice-cream and threw it to him. Murphy swallowed this, without it even touching the sides of his mouth, got up, wagged his tail and came back to us. I went over to the ice-cream vendor to thank him and to offer to pay for the ice-cream, but he said: 'No, you don't have to. The dog and I have an arrangement. The first day we were here he smelt the ice-cream, jumped up, put a paw either side of the opening and the caravan nearly fell over under his weight. Now we give him an ice-cream, he doesn't push us over and the K-9 protection racket works well'.

We also had another dog – a black Labrador called Satan. Satan, unlike Murphy, did not relish ice-cream but he loved the cornet in which the ice-cream was contained. The dogs developed a double-act. Sometimes, Murphy took Satan with him. They would walk up behind some child waving a cornet around and Murphy would neatly pluck the ice-cream out of the top. The child would look round and, seeing this huge shaggy animal, would scream and drop the cornet which Satan would pick up. So both were happy! It cost me a fortune in replacement ice-creams.

The third dog of the pack was a very small Jack Russell called Muppet. She was terrified of thunder and one day – at that stage my practice was at home – a patient was dropped off by taxi at the start of a thunder-storm. Muppet, frightened as usual and seeing an open door, fled, hopped into the taxi and settled down in the back.

The taxi driver apparently noticed her presence soon after, but for some reason failed to put two-and-two together. Instead of bringing her back to us, he took her to the police station. When we finally collected her we found that not only had he taken her to the police station, but he had charged for the taxi run. Her fear of thunder cost £3.50 – and she was told in future to go by bus!

One last Murphy story. We had some friends who stayed with us regularly. One, the husband, was a colleague of mine doing some training with me. Two, his wife, was a very petite American who, while being a great help at teaching the children to ride, was not very good at contributing to the general input of housework at the weekends, especially Sunday mornings.

One morning when everybody was at breakfast and she had not arrived, her husband Rick said 'Well, let's start without her'. We finished our breakfast and were clearing away with everybody thinking it would teach her a lesson, when Rick went to wake her up. On opening the bedroom door he found that Murphy had jumped on top of her while she was lying in the bed, pinned her down with the duvet tight around her (she weighed six-and-a-half stone, he weighed fifteen-and-a-half) and was gently huffing dog's breath in her face.

Apparently, every time she had opened her mouth to call for help, he had given her a lovely smacking French kiss which somewhat discouraged her from trying again. She had been pinned there for some seventy minutes because Murphy was very comfortable and would not move. She never came down late for breakfast again!

Terry Moule

Sit – good girl!

When my granddaughter, Samantha, was about two, she loved coming out with me and my dog, Ben, to buy the newspaper.

When we reached the kerb, I gave Ben the command to sit. When he did not respond, I repeated 'Sit' again very firmly. I turned to see what the tug was on my other hand to find Samantha obediently sitting on the kerb!

Jan King

Eat your hat!

I am President of our local WI, and a while ago our group organized a Fun Evening and I had to come up with an idea for a hat depicting a town. My idea was ingenious – Chippenham – guessed quite quickly by the members – I can't think why! Blue straw hat (bought for a wedding) with the addition of labels off two well-known brands of ham stuck around the crown, and micro-waved chips hanging from bits of string around the brim.

Heady with my success, I decided to keep the hat as a topic of conversation for when my grandchildren came to stay. Putting it carefully in the spare room, I firmly shut the door – or so I thought. One day, I went upstairs with my duster and vacuum cleaner and began picking up little bits of ? I wasn't quite sure what for a moment. But then I saw my hat with string hanging and not a single chip in sight. I had thought I had microwaved the chips until they were rock-solid. Penny, our Westie, obviously thought otherwise.

Marian Beale

Eggs away

When we were first married we lived in a caravan in a field belonging to a farmer. One day Rocky, our yellow Labrador, leapt into the caravan wagging his tail – and body – vigorously, with his mouth slightly open and orange-shaped. Placing my hand under his mouth I asked him to 'give' and he promptly put a hen's egg into my hand. I patted his head, told him he was a good boy and gave him a reward. The egg was in perfect condition, no cracks.

This event, since the hens were free range and laid their eggs all over the place, became a daily occurrence.

One day Rocky did his usual trick, gave me the egg but refused the reward. I then noticed that he had a further egg in his mouth. He had carried both eggs together and neither of them was broken. Needless to say, we had to stop this little game or pay the farmer for the eggs.

Mrs Olwyn Allen

TERRIBLE PETS

Road rage!

We were in the habit of leaving our dog, Monty, in the car outside a shop, and he would start barking as soon as we entered it. Fortunately, we couldn't hear him once we were inside doing what we had to do. We were, however, dismayed, when a lady came in and asked in a loud voice that caused all the other customers to turn and look 'Does anyone here own the car with the dog in it?' We dutifully owned up, expecting the usual comments that we should not leave the dog in the car, but, instead, she asked us to come outside. All the people in the shop came outside and looked, too.

There was Monty sitting in the driver's seat, obviously tired of barking, and intermittently pressing the horn instead. This, I might add, is now a regular occurrence.

Ellen Levin

SK: Nag! Nag! Hot weather often results in tragedy for pets left in cars. *Please* remember to leave windows and sun-roof ajar and a bowl of water for your pet.

Anyone for dogs and ladders?

As a young man, my father had a devoted black Labrador called Monty and, when he was on leave from doing his National Service, Monty, having been deprived of his beloved master's company for several months, spent the whole day glued to my father's side.

At the time, my grandmother was also looking after several of her nieces and nephews who were delighted to see their older cousin and pestering him at regular intervals throughout the days.

A problem with roof-tiles required my father's presence on the roof. He duly set up the ladder, climbed to the top and started work. At various times when he was standing on the top rungs of the ladder, the ladder was shaken from below. Eventually he called over his shoulder to his mother, insisting that she stop the children playing at the foot of the ladder. No response, so he kept shouting. Then he turned to look down – no children, no mother – but, right behind him, on the ladder, tail vigorously wagging, was Monty, delighted that he had, at long last, managed to reach his master.

The climb up had apparently been simple – but getting Monty down was another matter. The only way this could be safely accomplished was by my father climbing on to the roof and coaxing Monty up and off the ladder to join him. For some reason, Monty was not exactly enthusiastic about this. Once there, however, my father could pick him up and carry him back down the ladder – not a simple feat since Monty was no small animal. Both lived to tell the tale!

Janice Griffith

Art lover

Vicky, our Springer Spaniel, is elderly, overweight and has failing eyesight, but she is an habitual glutton who still retains a keen sense of smell and good hearing – able to detect a cornflake drop on a carpet at a hundred yards.

After Christmas my art student son, for reasons best known only to him, decided to make a model of a dodo out of the Christmas turkey carcass (which was retrieved from a tree in the garden where it had been hanging for the birds for several weeks). This model, with the aid of wire coat-hangers, newspaper and bits of string was finally completed, photographed and stored in the garage. My son returned to college with the intention of taking it with him on his next visit when he was less overloaded with luggage.

What we failed to realize was that the minute particles of flesh that remained on the carcass were now very 'high' – and were soon detected by the very keen nostrils of Vicky.

On returning from a shopping trip I discovered Vicky looking extremely furtive and rating a good 9.9 on the 'Up-to-no-good' scale. I soon found to my horror that she had located Dodo, devoured the entire carcass, but drawn the line at the wire and bits of string – which was all that remained of my son's precious work of art.

Carol Vinciguerra

Rocky I and II

I: Rocky was a beautiful rough-haired English Collie, but, somehow or other, his brains never seemed to match his personal charm. Either he was thick, or he had a lousy memory. Turn your back, and at the first opportunity Rocky was off – missing – gone – vanished – leaving everyone searching frantically for him. He could never ever remember where he lived, so his usual trick was to tag on to someone and follow them to wherever they were going, relying on them to bring him back home, or to contact us or the police with information as to his current whereabouts.

This was normal procedure until, one day, when out on one of his escapades, the telephone rang, and a lady's voice at the other end of the line said, 'Mr Peel? This is the convent. I believe we have your dog. Could you, please, come and collect him?'

From then on, this became a regular occurrence – Rocky had got religion. The Mother Superior, poor soul, must have added our number to the automatic dialling system of her telephone. Eventually, the 'phone would ring and the voice would say 'It's Sister Agnes. Rocky has had his lunch. Could he come home now?'

II: This behaviour continued until we moved to our present home - a new house on a new estate. As you know, all new estates look the same – lots of houses in various stages of completion, muddy roads and gardens like bomb-sites, each plot of land being marked out with two-by-two posts about two-feet-six stuck in the ground and a length of two-by-two nailed along the top of them. Such was the situation when, about a week or so after moving in, we were awakened in the very early hours of the morning by a great barking commotion. Freda, my wife, thinking that Rocky had been caught short, so to speak, popped her slippers on and went downstairs in her night attire – a pair of pants and one of my T-shirts.

Having let the dog out, Freda then realized that Rocky was not in need of a call of nature, but intent on seeing off an intruder – a cat. Not wanting to awaken the whole neighbourhood by yelling at

Rocky, Freda decided that the only thing to do was to set off after him and bring him back. You can imagine the scene, the cat haring up the gardens with Rocky in hot pursuit, followed by Freda, in T-shirt and pants, doing the high hurdles in the rain.

Unfortunately, unknown to Freda, someone, about four plots further up, had made a start on their garden, removing all the builder's rubble and making the best of what topsoil was available. This meant that, at this fence, the take-off side was higher than the landing side. At this point Freda came to grief, going A-over-H into the hole on the other side.

Eventually, Rocky was led home by his pursuer, who was covered in muck and manure, and making all kinds of threats, and generally casting aspersions on the dog's parentage.

Mr Peel

Caught in the act

A few years ago I had a very naughty dog called Sam. On this particular occasion, on arrival home from work, my neighbour called me into the garden.

'Sam,' she said, 'has been in my fridge in the garage.'

They had two fridges, and the overflow was in the garage for defrosting, which was why the door was left slightly ajar.

'Oh, what's he done now?' I asked nervously.

'Stolen some ham I was defrosting,' she replied.

'How do you know it was Sam?' I asked defensively.

'Because his paw-print is in the butter!' she said triumphantly.

Jackie Hall

Seeing stars!

While on a camping holiday I slept on a camp-bed in the lounge area of the tent as the bedroom area was full of the rest of the family. One night, while lying on my camp-bed, with our two dogs tied to my ankles to ensure they did not stray, a noise was heard outside. Gemma the faithful guard dog and Fred Boxer the dim-witted back-up awoke and listened to decide if action was needed. The next few seconds went so fast I am not sure what happened but, from lying asleep on the bed, I next found myself outside the tent, looking up at the night sky, the dogs still attached to my ankles.

Thankfully no-one had been about to see me being yanked under the tent door and dragged unceremoniously into the out-field, so I quickly tried to nip back in, but saw more stars as I hit the un-zipped door. Ouch!

Miss S. M. Horniblow

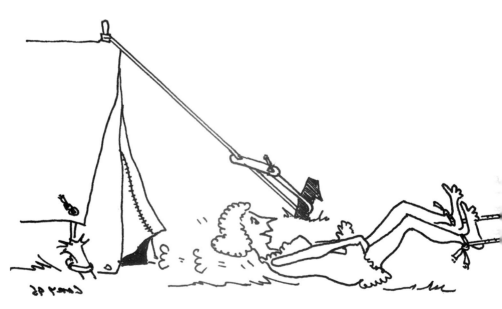

Taxi!

We once had a large, powerful, friendly yellow Labrador, called Winston, who just knew that everybody loved him! One day, after a great day on the beach, we were heading back to the car park, with my friend in charge of Winston on his lead.

Unfortunately, one of Winston's great joys was riding in cars. As the day was hot, there was a gentleman seated in the front passenger-seat of his car, reading his paper, with the door opened. Seconds later, I heard a surprised cry. Looking round, I saw that Winston had dived into the car, and gone straight through the newspaper on to the driver's seat. The startled cry was from my friend, who, still clutching the lead, was now lying in the lap of a gentleman, with a very amazed look on his face.

Sheila Rapley

One for the birds

Benji, our Jack Russell (long legs and shaggy coat) spends many hours sitting looking down the garden watching the birds. We encourage the birds in and provide water and food regularly. When Benji was younger he jealously chased them away, but now, at thirteen years old and a diabetic, he tolerates them. Well, we thought he did, until we saw him walk over to the birds' drinking water, lift his leg and, with perfect aim, top up the contents.

Patricia van Os

I say this is fun

We have a lovely Labrador, called Bach, eighteen weeks old. One day last week he made a mess on the garden path, so my husband pulled out the garden hose to clear it up, laid the hose on the path, and went round the corner to turn the water full on. By the time he came back to clear up the mess, Bach had picked up the end of the hose in his mouth and run through the kitchen and the lounge, watering, watering everywhere.

Trouble is, it's very hard trying to tell a dog off when you are falling about laughing.

Jeannine Terran

99 please

Years ago my Mum and Dad ran a small hotel at Woolacombe, North Devon. We were very busy in the summer months and our beloved Spaniel 'Mr Chips' did not, perhaps, get all the attention he wanted some days. One evening a guest said, 'Your dog looks just like the one down at the 'Red Barn' (the local ice-cream parlour/café). He did – he was the same dog! We soon discovered that Mr Chips was turning over his water bowl, a small enamelled pudding basin, and carrying it the mile along the front to the café. He then went from table to table sitting begging for ices which he got!

Lynda Fraser

Waste not, want not

My grandmother, who was staying with us, was in the kitchen preparing a plaice fillet for her lunch. All of a sudden we heard an anguished cry – Micky, the cat, had run off with the plaice. Tony, the terrier, dashed into the kitchen and chased the cat over several gardens. Five minutes later he returned, head held high, and dropped the very muddy fish at my grandmother's feet. Being a very Victorian lady of the waste-not-want-not brigade, she washed the plaice and then continued to prepare and cook it for her lunch.

Mrs Kathy Smith

Magnificent obsession

My parents had a miniature Yorkshire Terrier, who was a compulsive thief. This particular morning we sent Minty upstairs to wake my father who doted on him. My mother and I were standing at the bottom of the stairs by the front door talking, when Minty, his beady little eyes gleaming triumphantly, appeared at the top of the stairs with the bottom set of dad's false teeth dangling from his mouth.

Because he was so small, he could not see the stairs over the teeth and tumbled down, squeaking on contact with each stair. Then, with his jaws still firmly clenching the teeth, he hit the front door with a thud. Mum and I tried to out-wit him by cutting off his escape and trapping him behind the sofa, but we were no match for this artful dodger who ricocheted off the cushions, sprinted through the kitchen and deftly popped out through the cat-flap.

'Quick,' stammered my mother breathlessly, 'watch to see where he buries them.'

After making three attempts to put us off the trail, Minty finally settled on a spot under the rose bushes.

Half-an-hour later, my father came down, oblivious to the commotion, and asked gumily: 'Doreen, have you seen my teeth?' 'You left them down here last night, dear,' she replied with Oscar-winning normality, and pointed to the hurriedly exhumed and washed teeth! Months later – and only after Dad had had a couple of pints – we told him the truth.

By the way, while digging up the teeth we came across a pair of tights, two pens, umpteen soggy tissues, and an equally damp five-pound note!

On another occasion Minty's zest for stealing was revived when he spotted a nest of small kittens apparently abandoned under a bush in his garden. One by one he carefully transported the kittens through our cat-flap and into his warm cosy basket in the kitchen. Mother, bleary eyed, entered and proceeded to go about making breakfast. As she turned and headed for the fridge, small writhings from inside

Minty's basket caught the corner of her eye. Suddenly, wide awake, her piercing screams reached the rest of the household who came running convinced she was being murdered.

Dad was the first to arrive on the scene which now comprised Mother standing on top of the worktop, pressed against the wall, shaking and pointing an unsteady finger at Minty's basket. 'Rats,' she stammered. Just then, Minty popped in through the cat-flap with the last of his charges dangling from his mouth, followed by the irate mother of the litter.

To this day, Mum still cannot recall how she managed to get up on to the worktop.

Minty went broody after that, so we bought him a couple of small fluffy toys which he alternately mothered, beat up, hid and made love to, depending on his mood!

Vivienne Tregidga

Feeling peckish!

Our old Labrador, Anna, frequently opens the fridge when left on her own, helping herself to whatever she fancies. On one occasion we returned to find her sitting very sheepishly in her bed, not wanting to look at us because the fridge door was open, an empty plate was on the kitchen floor, and there was no sign of the roast beef. When she was a puppy, she also ate a pound note which had been left on the table.

We also have a cat who frequently comes into the kitchen, opens the fridge and looks in to see what she fancies.

We now keep a chair in front of the fridge!

Paula Whitehouse

TERRIBLE PETS

How much is it worth?

I had never been very fond of dogs and I still can't bear cats! However, when my next door neighbour was ill, I offered to do some cleaning for her, even though she had a Spaniel, called Jessica, which she asked me to let out mid-morning. A bit afraid of handling Jessica, I hit upon the idea of opening the garden door and throwing a biscuit out-side for her to follow. She did, so all was well! However, when I tried the same trick the next week, Jessica came and stood on my feet! As she was much heavier than me I couldn't move and was pinned to the floor. Eventually, I managed to twist myself round and reach for the biscuits. I threw one into the garden, but she still didn't move. She just looked at me as if to say 'You'll have to do a lot better than that'. So, I threw several more biscuits, but without success. Finally, I showed her the empty tin. At that point, she grinned, got off my feet, walked casually off into the garden and ran round gobbling up all the biscuits.

Olive Gregson

Ginger nutter

Some years ago we 'adopted' a stray greyhound from the RSPCA. His mission in life was to devour everything which was vaguely edible, be it fruit, veg, flesh or fowl, raw or cooked, fresh or decomposing, it mattered not one jot to our Louis.

In our village was a small branch of Lloyds Bank with very friendly cashiers. I always combined my visits to the bank with Louis' lunch-time 'walkies', and he was regularly treated to a couple of ginger biscuits by the staff who would push the treats under the security screen for him. On one occasion, however, the exchange of a large canvas bag of change meant that the security screen was opened up for a moment. Presumably Louis imagined this to be the entrance to some ginger-nut paradise. Before I could gather my senses, he had sprung from the floor, through the security screen and landed on all fours in the cash scoop. Fortunately I had enough tension on the lead to prevent him completing his trajectory into the lap of the surprised cashier.

Not even the most dog-loving person would relish the sudden descent of a fully grown, ginger-nut-crazed greyhound on to their person during normal banking hours!

Mrs Margaret Stokes

MIAOWS

Milking the milkman dry

My small white cat was absolutely convinced it was a Retriever and constantly staggered home with assorted trophies, such as balls of wool, clothes pegs, bits of paper, and so on and on.

One day I was asking our replacement milkman what had happened to his predecessor, and was told he had had a nervous breakdown. Soon, while spring-cleaning the cat's bed in the broom cupboard, I found out why. Under the dust-sheets, obviously collected on the cat's early-morning rounds, was a pile of crumpled notes bearing messages: 'No milk today.' 'One-dozen eggs, please.' 'Away all next week.' And so on, and so on, and…

Please omit my surname in case the milkman or members of his family read this!

Alison

Pussy galore

We once had a black cat called Mickey. Or, to be more precise, He had Us.

After about ten years of his company, I responded to a ring at the door to find a neighbour, from a few doors down, asking if we could do them a favour and feed their cat while they were on holiday. The more we got chatting about their cat and its likes and dislikes, the more it sunk in that it was no coincidence that it sounded exactly like our cat, Mickey. It was not a clone – it was the same cat.

All those years, Mickey had eaten heartily at our house, had a good sleep by the fire, then took himself off and had dinner No 2. We would never have cottoned on if our neighbours had not knocked on our door. And Mickey lived for twenty-one years. How many dinners is that…

Mike Sammes

Cat burglar

In the 1970s, I had a pet Staffie/Corgi cross-breed named Cymru, and a cat named Sasha – a stray that had adopted my father and me. At the time, I did shift-work and, one afternoon, I woke with a start unsure what had woken me. I had left the radio playing quietly downstairs and knew my father was out for the day, but as I lay gathering my senses I could hear movements. I listened carefully. The sounds were definitely not coming from the radio, but from the spare room at the end of the passage.

With thoughts of intruders looming large – there had been a spate of daytime break-ins recently – I crept as silently as I could to my half-opened bedroom door. I am a born coward, but I was concerned for Cymru and Sasha whom I had left sleeping soundly in the living-room. As I listened nervously, another bumping scraping sound came from the spare room. I peered out into the passage and saw Cymru sitting perfectly still by the spare-room door staring intently inside as if she were watching something. The hairs on the back of my neck stood on end – intruders! Another sound came from the room, and, at that moment, Cymru, obviously pleased, tail-wagging, pushed open the door and entered. Realizing by now that it must be Sasha in the room, I breathed a deep sigh of relief and went to see what they were up to. As I approached I heard a 'splat' noise and, a few seconds later, another 'splat'. I crept up to the door and looked in.

Sasha was on top of a cupboard where I kept a tray of fresh eggs that a friend brought me from her own chickens every other week. As I stood watching, she carefully hooked another egg from the tray with her paw, tapped it to the edge of the cupboard, then edged it over to join its shattered companions on the floor where Cymru was sitting patiently waiting. 'Splat'! When this egg landed, Sasha jumped down and both animals fell to, eating the raw eggs (and shells!) with great enjoyment.

At last, the mystery of the missing eggs was solved (I had earlier on accused my father of using (or breaking) eggs without telling me).

When I pushed open the spare-room door, saying loudly, 'What are you two up to?', two guilty faces, dripping raw egg, looked up at me startled. Then Sasha, with great dignity, stalked past me and made her way, tail swishing downstairs. Cymru, always a glutton, snatched a last mouthful of shell and then scampered past me, crunching away like mad. By the time I got downstairs they were both pretending to be asleep in their usual places on opposite sides of the living-room.

Miss Barbara E. Owen

Stray cat

Oh, what unhappy twist of fate
Has brought you homeless to my gate?
The gate where once another stood
To beg for shelter, warmth and food.
For from that day I ceased to be
The master of my destiny.

While he, with purr and velvet paw
Became within my house, The Law.
He scratched the furniture and shed,
And claimed the middle of my bed.
He ruled in arrogance and pride,
And broke my heart the day he died.

So if you really think, Oh Cat,
I'd willingly relive all that
Because you come, forlorn and thin
Well – don't just stand there – come on in!

Francis Witham

Take that, you

About three years ago, in the middle of summer, during a very hot spell when very little night-clothing was being worn, our cat was having a howling match about two a.m., beneath our bedroom window. My husband, not wearing much – in view of the hot weather – got up, went down and out into the garden to grab the cat.

Meanwhile, not realizing he had got out of bed, I, too, got up, went to the bathroom, filled a container with cold water, carried it back, and threw it out of the window at the precise moment my husband made a wild grab at the cat. The cat ran off, the security light came on, and my husband, drenched in cold water, stood illuminated by the light.

We now keep a loaded water pistol on the windowsill.

Mrs N. Nessham

Pets wanted

My dear mother, now in her late seventies, fainted in Hammersmith Post Office and was promptly whipped off by ambulance to nearby Charing Cross Hospital. My mother has an irrational fear of hospitals and as soon as she was able and, in spite of all the entreaties of the staff, she discharged herself, giving as the reason the totally fictitious need to 'feed her cat and three kittens' shut up at home.

Greatly concerned for her wellbeing, the hospital telephoned my brother to ask him to get Mother back to them without delay after she had 'fed her pets'. Not wishing to expose his mother in a lie, he helpfully confirmed that she would, of course, be very worried about her 'two little dogs'.

Maggie Ferrari

Perfect timing

Some years ago, when we lived in Macclesfield, we invited a couple in the next street for dinner one night. Things went well: Chanette being a great cook had done us proud, and the three-course banquet was greatly appreciated by all.

After the meal, we adjourned to the easy chairs, and brandies, and generally chatted, as you do. The couple told us about their favourite Sunday lunch – leg-of-lamb roast, with garlic, and the usual vegetables. Apparently, on one occasion, after carving the lamb, and dishing up the veggies, they had left the lamb on the window ledge to cool while they set about the first course in the dining room. Suddenly the sound of breaking crockery alerted them, and, upon entering the kitchen, they caught sight of an enormous black cat, with leg-of-lamb, disappearing through the window – never to be seen again.

It was at this point in the tale, when Tiddles, our rather large adventurous cat, woke up, thudded downstairs on her leaden feet and made her appearance in the lounge.

Simultaneously our guests pointed at Tiddles, and, in perfect harmony, screamed 'That's the cat!'

As we all know, animals have a great sense of timing, and Tiddles certainly proved that point, that night!

Brian Burgess

In the pink!

My friend has a cat called Kitty. When I write to her using a pink envelope, Kitty hooks out the 'pinkie' from the rest of the mail and sits on it. When I run out of pink envelopes and use blue, cream or white envelopes, she is not in the slightest bit interested. So, just imagine three OAPs scouring the shops of Farnham, Midhurst and Chichester for pink envelopes to please a cat!

Mrs Sylvia Pett

Wandering star!

We live on a retirement complex of sixty flats and one of our rules is 'no pets'. One pretty black-and-white cat, however, cares nothing for rules and regularly strolls around the complex en route to her 'wash room' on a bit of waste ground nearby.

All the residents know her, and enjoy stroking her as she goes by. She sits very demurely while the ladies stroke her, but rolls over, like a wanton hussy!, on her back, offering her fluffy tummy to the men.

She often enjoys sitting in our porch soaking up the sun during the day, but we never saw her after dark, until one bitterly cold night we found her sleeping there. Worried that maybe her owners had gone away and deserted her, we took her in (just for the night you understand) until we could find out where she lived. She immediately snuggled down on my husband's lap, purring and looking very smug.

Next day, we discovered that, far from being homeless or deserted, she lived in a lovely home with nice people and two other cats, both younger than she was. Mitzi, as we now know she is called, is an elderly cat and it seems she prefers to be in elderly company. Her young 'mum' told us that, in the last five years, she has tried to move in with no less than five other elderly residents and that she has perfected her lost-and-hungry look. Just for the moment, we were her favourites so, with her owner's consent, she continued to sit on our porch all day and, once a day, my husband would walk her back to her house, with Mitzi trotting behind him like a dog. On arrival, she would pop in through the cat-flap, grant her owners half-an-hour of her time, then return to our porch. We have all heard of 'Pat' dogs, but this 'Stroke' cat certainly gives us all a lot of pleasure.

Yesterday, we didn't see much of her. Then, as the district nurse was passing, she called out 'If you are looking for Mitzi, she is sitting with Rose in her flat'. So, perhaps, we have had our turn. But we do hope she will still look in when passing. She probably knows Rose isn't too well, and that she needs her company more than we do.

Joyce Gillham

Come home, Choky

My son and his family live in a small Close where most of the gardens are open plan, and most of the houses have cat-flaps. My son had two tabby cats, a brother and sister called Ludvig and Choky, who were totally inseparable – that is, until the new baby arrived and Choky decided to leave home and move in with a family a little further down the Close.

After many attempts to get her to return – and a lot of heart-searching – it was decided to let her remain there. A few days passed and then, one morning on his way to the garage, Simon noticed something rather familiar (his pants) on the pavement. With a some-what red face he picked them up, popped them into the hall, and then went off to work with just a passing thought.

That evening his wife asked how a strange bra came to be on the hall carpet. Simon denied all knowledge, of course. Next day he found a pair of his socks on the lawn, followed by various other items of underwear as the week progressed. Then, on the Saturday morning, Choky's new mum came to the house with a small pile of clean cloth-ing that she had kindly washed after Ludvig had carried it in his mouth along the road and through the cat-flap – sometimes dropping items on the way.

We decided that he was so confused by his sister now living in a different house that he was slowly moving the old house to her! Everything eventually calmed down, and the only thing that Ludvig takes to our neighbours now is the occasional mouse. As long as he takes it to Choky and not from her to us, that's okay with us!

Anon

Toad in the hall

I have two cats. One is a regular hunter, doing what comes naturally. The other one, Meggy, is much gentler. She likes to stalk, catch and bring indoors, but does not kill. On one occasion the family were out and I thought I would have a luxurious bath, lots of hot water and a book. I was wallowing happily when I heard a loud squeal. I froze. What on earth was it? Silence. Then another squeal.

I leapt out of the bath, donned a skimpy bath-towel and rushed downstairs thinking that perhaps one of the cats had been hurt in some way. But, oh no. Meggy had brought in the most enormous toad who was lying on the hall carpet, on his back, squealing his head off. When I approached him he played dead, deflating unbelievably. I picked him up and examined him to make sure he had not been hurt and then gently ran him under the tap. This obviously revived him and he hopped off quite happily when I put him back into the deepest jungle part of the garden.

On another occasion I 'lost' a mouse in the hall. Meggy had brought it in, but it managed to escape into the minutest of cracks and I just couldn't find it. I did a couple of days later, though – in my garden shoes when I went to put them on!

Gill Turner

Anyone for pheasant?

If our cat Delphi could talk, she probably wouldn't even bother to speak to the sort of people she has condescended to live with for her fifteen summers.

When she was a lithe Siamese-kittenish one-year-old, I fitted a cat-flap to the kitchen door to let her come and go at will. One Saturday morning, my wife, Sue, and I were attracted by sounds of scuffling at the flap and went to see what the problem might be. There was Delphi, half-way through the flap, struggling to pull a twice-her-size pheasant through after her.

Just where the pheasant had come from we had no idea but, as we live near a field and the bird was quite cold, we assumed she must have picked it up from there. Fearing that it might have died from poisoning we reluctantly put it deep in the dustbin and firmly put the lid on.

Minutes later – there was more scuffling at the cat-flap. On investigation, we found the wretched cat back again with the bird. How on earth had she got into the dustbin? Risking life and limb, we again dragged the pheasant from an exceedingly angry cat, opened the bin only to find the first bird still in place!

Our puzzlement over the incident lasted for several months until the day a neighbour was overheard at a party, describing how thieves had broken into his garage and stolen a brace of pheasants.

Obviously a cat-burglar!

Ray G. Davies

43

Fair catch!

When I was ten, we had a lively black-and-white cat, called Monty, who loved to sit on top of our wireless set, because of the warmth. As the wireless was on a shelf, this also gave him a commanding view of the room.

The Insurance Man (who we were fairly sure was bald and wore a toupee) used to call every Friday night. One evening when he arrived, Monty, in very skittish mood, had retreated to his usual place atop the wireless from whence he glared down at everyone. The Insurance Man's head bobbed around as he talked, and Monty, seeing the animated toupee, crouched menacingly and then leapt! The toupee was off in a trice, and Monty retreated upstairs with it, hiding under a bed and growling fiercely, as cats do, when anyone tries to deprive them of their prize.

Eventually Monty was lured from his retreat with a plate of fish, and our Insurance Man was able to continue his round with his toupee – but not his dignity – restored. Fortunately, he moved to another district a few months later.

Graeme and Elizabeth Young

A budding make-up artiste?

When my daughter, Zoe, was about three, we had visitors to dinner – her Aunt and Uncle. After the meal, Zoe left the table and, while we were chatting, things were very quiet elsewhere! We suddenly realized this and called out 'Zoe, what are you doing?' As there was no response, we thought it prudent to investigate.

Walking into our lounge, we found that she had plundered her Aunt's handbag of all its goodies, had cut all the whiskers off Sandy, our ginger tom – and, for good measure, had smothered him, herself, the settee and the carpet with lipstick.

We still do not know how she managed to hold the cat still and cut off all his whiskers, but whiskerless he was for a very long time.

Carole Mayhod

Very fetching!

When I came into the kitchen to find bright yellow feathers covering the floor, I thought my cat, Jenny, had caught an exotic bird. Thankfully, it was only a feather duster, but where had it come from? I had never bought a feather duster.

Periodically, after that, Jenny would arrive home with one in her mouth. Eventually I traced the source – along the main road, through automatic doors, pass J. Sainsbury, and into the shopping mall! There, outside the cane shop, was a basket of feather dusters! Some friends, who worked in Sainsbury's, later told us they had witnessed Jenny trotting back along the main road with a feather duster! Shamefully, I did not offer to pay for the dusters, but, from then on, I made sure she had her own supply.

When we moved into the country she took up fishing – jumping into a neighbours' pond and bringing home her catch. I would then put the catch in a bucket and return it. To his credit, the neighbour was never cross. 'She always comes to help me feed the fish, you know,' he said calmly. 'She is such a sweetie'. Not the word I would use for her!

Sadly, Jenny has long since gone to pussy-cat heaven – she lost while playing a game of 'chicken' with a tipper truck.

Sue Salt

TERRIBLE PETS

Very fishy!

In the early 1930s I lived with my mother in a bed-sit in London. One Sunday my aunt and uncle were coming to tea, and, as a special treat, my mother had bought my uncle a pint of shrimps, and left them in the bag on the draining board while we walked to meet our visitors.

When we returned for tea, there were no shrimps – no bag – no nothing. We were all mystified, and, as at the time, we had a pet kitten we all looked very suspiciously at her. I cannot remember now what we had for tea, but it certainly wasn't shrimps. Over the next week, however, the shrimps re-appeared – under rugs, behind curtains, in the beds, under pillows and behind cushions. You name it, the kitten had hidden one there – even the rolled-up bag in which the shrimps had been. For days, there was a very fishy smell.

Mrs B. J. Tye

A case of mistaken identity

We have always had several cats and, two years ago, new neighbours and their two cats moved into the house backing on to ours. One of their cats – Willow – is a very beautiful Oriental cat, but a terrible bully. He got into the habit of coming into our house and chasing our three cats. One of them, Dougal, had always been a bit of a wimp (a coward, to be honest) and Willow used to pick on him in particular. It got to the stage where there was open warfare under our bed in the early hours with a lot of bad feline language.

We regularly chased Willow out and tried various means of discouraging him, including several nights with me shouting phrases such as: 'Will you get out right now.' 'Don't you dare come back in here again.' 'Your behaviour is absolutely disgraceful.' 'GET OUT NOW' – etc.

Then my long-suffering husband pointed out that, as no names were ever mentioned, it was very possible that the neighbours were getting the wrong end of the stick and that was why he was getting such very strange looks.

Eileen Hodder

TERRIBLE PETS

Picture this

Some years ago, my husband, an ardent 'Western' viewer, settled himself down for two hours of vintage John Wayne, with, as always, our cat, Archie, draped in his favourite spot across the top of the TV.

On this occasion, without any warning, Archie suddenly deposited the contents of his stomach all over the screen – and, yes, into the works at the back. Everything stopped and went silent – except for the unprintable expletives from my husband.

The following morning I phoned the rental firm and asked for an engineer to call. 'What seems to be the trouble?' said a robotic voice. 'My cat has been sick in the tele,' I replied. About two minutes passed, then a slightly more interested voice said: 'We haven't come across this problem before. Do you have a picture?'

Needless to say we required a new TV and, if my husband had had his way, a new cat.

Pat Williams

Teacher's pet

Last year my husband, a gardener, came across a tiny abandoned kitten which, much to the delight of our daughter, Beth, aged five, he brought home. Unfortunately the kitten, which Beth named Sooty, only survived for three days.

Trying to convert a very sad situation into a positive experience, we decided to have a garden burial and a prayer, explaining to Beth that Sooty had left his body behind and gone to heaven.

As we stood over the grave Beth remarked how she would have liked to take Sooty to school to show the class. 'You can't take kittens to school Beth,' I said, 'they would run away.' To which she replied, 'No, mummy. Not if it was dead. Hannah brought a starfish last week and that was dead.'

One wonders how teachers cope with what's presented for the nature table!

Margaret Durkin

SQUEAKS, SQUAWKS, HE-HAWS AND THUMPERS

What a nerve!

All through the summer, when we open our front door, the following happens. After the seagulls have eaten our cats' food, they walk across the lawn and wash their beaks in the bird bath. One particular gull is so tame that he often walks right into the house, even when our five moggies are around, and eats the food off a saucer. Got to give him ten-out-of-ten for nerve!

Mrs Joan Rowland

Road hog!

During the war my sister, then aged seventeen, and advised to have an outdoor job, became a milk-lady. This entailed getting up very early, of course, travelling to the milk-bottle loading point and getting her horse and cart. She had various horses to cope with over the years, but one in particular was named Gabby. He had the knack of disappearing while she was delivering the milk, and she would find him with his head in the pig-bins which were placed at various lamp posts in the roads at that time. He would knock the lids off and, despite having just had his breakfast, would search out tasty morsels. A certain lady was also in the habit of putting out crusts of bread for him and he would refuse to budge from her gatepost until he had a tit-bit. That was fine when she remembered, but...

His other 'trick' was when my sister took him into Bristol to be re-shod. He always knew when they were on their way home and used to go 'like the clappers' all through the main roads. The lights on the cart were two candles, one placed each side, in jam-jar like containers. The roads, fortunately for my sister and Gabby, were not so busy in those days.

Peggy Kieser

Humps and bumps in the night

While on a touring holiday, my husband and I stayed overnight in a farmhouse near Hereford. While my husband was in the bathroom I turned back the bed covers and, horror of horrors, three enormous black spiders scuttled out from a pillow sham. Frozen to the spot - as, indeed, were the spiders now on the bed cover - my husband eventually responded to my screams, grabbed an empty glass, and, in the time-honoured way, shook them, one by one, out of the window. Having also responded to my insistence that he strip the bed right down to the ticking, and then remake it, he fell exhausted into bed and persuaded me to undress and do likewise. As I stood trembling nervously in my nightie, we heard our hosts come to bed in the next room. Precisely at that moment I glanced down at the replaced, pleated, floor-length bed valance and let out a strangled scream as my worst fears were confirmed and I saw four - yes four - more enormous black hairy spiders.

'Good grief! Not more?' my exhausted husband cried out.

'More. More.' I hissed breathlessly back.

After further humping-thumping-bumping of bed linen and furniture during the second bout of bed-stripping, pillow-plumping, window-opening and shutting, and plus 'more-more' breathless shrieks from me as another spider made a bid for freedom, plus evermore exhausted despairing cries from my husband, he finally went to sleep while I sat up all night with the light on.

The next morning, despite our age (late fifties) it was only too clear that our hosts thought we had been on some kind of erotic escapade, and, needless to say, they carefully avoided asking us if we had slept well! Thank God, we had only booked in for one night.

Kathryn Harper

TERRIBLE PETS

Putting your foot in it

I had just had my kitchen re-done and was so pleased with the effect that I decided rather rashly that I would keep the surfaces totally clear. One morning I went shopping and, at the baker's, treated myself to a very large luscious strawberry-and-fresh-cream tart. I carried it home very carefully and put it gently next to the cooker, savouring the moment when I could eat it. But, as the washing machine had just finished, I took the clothes outside and hung them on the line. Unfortunately I had left the kitchen door open and when I got back all our hens were in the kitchen, and one was actually sitting in the sink! I pushed her out, but instead of just flying down she ran all the way round the beautifully cleaned U-shaped surfaces and, with the last step, put her foot right in the middle of my lovely cream cake!

Fortunately, my daughter's friend had a Saturday job in the bakery and the story made them laugh so much they sent me four more tarts.

Glennis Williams

Dog training

When Cockie, a cockatiel, first arrived our two dogs occasionally gave him a problem, but there was no doubt Cockie was 'top dog'. It sounded funny telling Cockie to leave a Labrador and a Collie-Cross alone. Then along came Ben, a two-year-old English Springer Spaniel, trained a little as a gun-dog. Try as he did, Cockie just could not make Ben toe-the-line like the other dogs.

One day Cockie was perched on the back of a chair cleaning himself when, with one leap, soon accompanied by much muffled squawking, Ben nabbed him, standing with Cockie's wings flapping from the side of his mouth. A sharp shout made him open his mouth and out came Cockie. Did Cockie panic? No! He hovered for a moment, then stuck his beak into Ben's nose before returning to the back of the chair to continue his ablutions.

Ben (now eleven years) has had a lot of respect for Cockie since then.

Phil and Ann Barnes

Swanning about

Walking along the sea-front between Clacton and Walton-on-Naze last summer with my sister-in-law we spotted a swan just out at sea. We always think of swans as stately birds, but this one had a sense of humour. It was surfing! It was swimming out several yards then turning and letting the waves carry it back to shore. It would then walk a few feet up the beach, turn round and do the same again.

Mrs Peggy Fairhall

Show me the way to go home

We lived in a house with small willow-type trees around the gardens (sorry, I'm hopeless with names). The leaves were getting very diseased, so we decided to cut the trees down. At that time we also made wine and had a very good wheat-wine fermenting. After we drained the wine off, we always put the waste on the 'heap' at the bottom of the garden.

The birds loved our trees, but they also loved the drained-off wheat! And, on this occasion, we had cut the trees down. So, there were all these drunken birds swooping and dive-bombing around with nowhere to land. It was the funniest sight I had seen – poor, drunken, bewildered birds staggering around looking for their usual perches.

Mrs Joan Penman

Bird bar – open

Many years ago, when we were first married, we used to make a lot of our own wines using fresh fruit, berries or flowers. After fermenting the 'must' for many days in a plastic dustbin bought specially for wine-making purposes, the seething bubbling mass had to be strained ready for racking into demi-johns, and the remaining fruit pulp disposed of. My husband then had the bright idea of putting a panful of fat juicy raisins on to his compost heap. Big mistake!

The garden was soon full of birds, all fighting for a place at the bar, swooping off in all directions, colliding in mid-air, hanging grimly on to the fence, falling from branches etc. The cat watched all this in amazement, but left the scene very suddenly when a drunken starling literally ran across the grass towards him squawking what we took to be 'Put 'em up, puddycat'.

It was a scene of complete mayhem and debauchery, and it was a very long time before the cat was able to look a bird in the eye again.

Kath Worts

TERRIBLE PETS

CARY 95

What a clever bunny am I

Several years ago we bought my eldest stepson a dwarf rabbit for his birthday, but the novelty soon wore off and he became my pet.

Our garden is not very large, mainly lawn with flower-beds around the sides. Whenever we could, we let the rabbit have the freedom of the garden and the resulting destruction of the plants was compensated for by the delightful playfulness of this little animal enjoying his freedom.

In time the rabbit became familiar with everything in the garden, and he would follow my husband around with eager curiosity whenever he was gardening.

One year my husband was busy planting daffodil bulbs, and, as usual, the rabbit was following him around. After much hard back-breaking work, my husband came in for a cup of tea.

After a while we both went out into the garden only to find all the daffodil bulbs lined up along the path, and one very smug-looking bunny standing nearby.

No, he didn't end up as rabbit pie and was sorely missed when he died in 1993. We have since taken in another rabbit from the RSPCA and are constantly surprised by the 'intelligence' and 'humour' of these delightful creatures.

Mrs Avril J. Hale

Smoke gets in your eyes

Our son, Richard, then aged about five, had a small hamster called Hammy. Unfortunately the hamster, an adventurer, was never happy in his beautiful cosy cage and was for ever escaping – especially at night which gave him a head start. Once he was missing for several days before being discovered in the tray under my gas cooker.

On another occasion, as we sat having our meal, we heard strange scratching noises overhead and realized he had gone off again. The bedroom was thoroughly investigated, but no Hammy was found. Then a small hole was discovered in the floorboards under a wardrobe and we could hear Hammy running backwards and forwards, limited only in his journeys by a joist beam which restricted him to one corner area of his underfloor kingdom.

Nothing could persuade him to come out and much frustration and a few youthful tears followed. Eventually the family retired downstairs leaving Dad to solve the problem.

We returned some time later to find the carpet rolled back, the wardrobe moved, one floorboard removed and Dad sitting cross-legged on the floor. He was puffing away at his pipe and blowing the resulting smoke down a small rubber tube into the space under the floorboards.

Shortly afterwards, amidst much laughter from us, a coughing, bewildered Hammy emerged and gave himself up. He lived a long time afterwards, but gave up adventuring!

Mrs Jean Earle

Get me out of here!

Maureen, a girl I work with, had been to the Animal Refuge and selected Tess, an Alsatian, about a year old. Tess lives in a kennel outside, but is allowed in the house when the family is at home.

Already living at the house is Oz, the hamster, who somehow got out of his cage. Maureen frantic, because her son, Andrew, would soon be home, was searching high and low. All of a sudden, as she was searching, the dog started to throw up. Maureen put Tess outside and was about to clean up the mess when the mess moved!

'Oh quick, Mike,' Maureen yelled, realizing what had happened. 'It's Oz. Put the poor thing out of its misery.'

Oz must have heard this because, when he moved again, he ran across the floor. By the time Maureen had caught him he was reasonably clean, but not very sweet-smelling!

Well, it's four days later now, and Oz, fed-and-watered, in his new abode well out of Tess's way, seems none the worse for his ordeal. We are all amazed that he is alive and well.

Lyn Charlton

The service is terrible here!

Grandma was sitting in the sunroom waiting for her breakfast, with Judy, our Trinidad parrot, keeping her company. Maybe I was a little late attending to them, but as I came through with the breakfast tray, Judy enunciated very clearly 'Ah fed up, you know. Ah fed up'.

Mrs J. W. Young

Drama queens!

A member of our animal-mad household is Sydney, a parrot, who used to send Muppet, our Jack Russell, into complete hysteria by first of all mewing at her like a cat, barking at her in her own bark, and finally throwing seed out of his bowl over her head.

Is it any wonder she didn't like birds?

Terry Moule

Operation ele

A baby elephant visited the Equine Clinic at the Animal Health Trust to make use of our X-ray machine – one of the most powerful in Europe. The Trust is designed for horses not elephants and, as the baby elephant was too large to fit into any of the stables, his bed for the night was one of our large, roomy, padded anaesthetic boxes. He quickly settled down, but as he was to have an operation the next day he had not been fed and woke up very hungry in the small hours of the morning.

In his quest for food he managed to force open the doors of the anaesthetic box and get into the operating theatre. He had a whale of a time exploring before his crashing around alerted the duty vet. Anyone who says bulls in china shops cause damage, should see the effects of an elephant in an operating theatre!

Phil Spiby

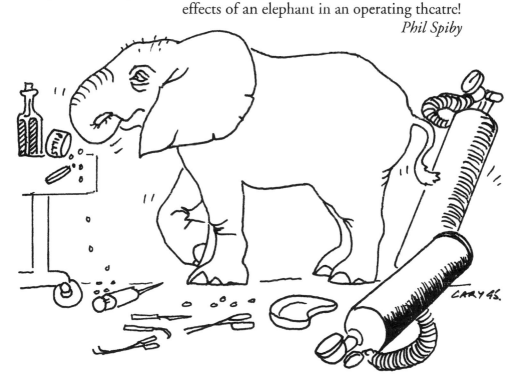

Who am I?

My two daughters, when young, had a rabbit. One does not think of rabbits as being particularly entertaining, but Bungey was quite a character.

During the summer he used to entertain his friends – mostly sparrows and the odd robin – to tea in his hutch; they would pop in through the wire-mesh at the front and peck about among the cereal and seeds while he sat watching benignly.

On cold winter nights, however, he had a box in the corner of the kitchen and it was then that his true character emerged – Bungey thought he was a dog! His favourite trick was to hop around the kitchen picking up stray shoes (even wooden exercise sandals) one at a time in his mouth and taking them back to his box, where he would pile up his trophies, looking very pleased with himself. Fluffy slippers sent him into a frenzy – we think he thought they were lady rabbits – and anyone wearing them could find a loudly grunting passionate (oh, yes, they do) rabbit clinging lovingly to their foot.

At breakfast time, as soon as he smelt toast cooking, he would sit up very straight in his box, ears erect, and everyone, including visitors, would be expected to contribute a finger of toast. Bungey would 'beg' on his haunches like a dog, snatch the toast before you could change your mind, then, turning his back on you, crunch it ecstatically.

He enjoyed the company of other animals, although he was not too keen on having his ears washed by one of my daughter's cats, and was often seen sitting with his front paws resting on a recumbent dog.

Jacky Lewis

SK: I particularly like Bungey's attitude to life!

A wing and a prayer!

We had been looking after my in-laws' Orange Canary who had never sung since the day they bought it. My daughter was changing his drinking water when the canary had escaped and headed for the open patio doors. As it went to fly outside, Buster, our Cocker Spaniel, leapt up and caught it in his mouth. I looked out into the garden and saw Buster running around the garden with the head of the bird sticking out of his mouth. I set off in pursuit.

Finally Buster ran back indoors, went under the dining-room table and deposited the bird on the carpet. Although it was still breathing I did not expect it to last long. I placed it back in the cage and we all went off to Church. We came home expecting the canary to be feet upwards at the bottom of the cage, but no! It was sitting on its perch singing away for all it was worth.

Vincent Carrington

SK: Bit of excitement does a bird good.

I like it here!

When our son Philip was three years old my then husband and I rescued a donkey foal that was being neglected and in need of some tender loving care. He was only about eight weeks old with small body, long gangly legs and enormous ears, so we called him Dillan after the rabbit on *Magic Roundabout*.

We fenced off half our garden to give him a nice paddock and built him a cedar wood stable. An ideal pet for Philip to grow up with, we thought! Our house has a small lane up one side and the local children regularly called in to see Dillan on their way home from school, bringing him peppermints and apples. Thus began the creation of a very spoiled donkey. His first year with us was one of drought, and hay was pretty scarce. Now donkeys are supposed to be excellent for clearing rough grazing and eating thistle hay, so say the books, but not Dillan. We got so worried about his refusal to eat what the book said he would eat that we went to beg a local race-horse breeder to sell us his best hay!

We also bought a head-collar to take him out for walks, but Dillan's favourite activity was to drop his head and bite you in the thigh, and while you hopped on one leg in excruciating pain, he would then make a bid for freedom and bolt for it. Although he was only young he was very strong and it always took a few hundred yards to get him back under control.

He loved human company so when we were out gardening we let him out of his paddock to join us. One day, while we were otherwise engaged in the garden, he went missing. We searched everywhere. Thinking someone had left a garden gate open we even searched the streets, but no Dillan. It was only when I was walking disconsolately up the drive towards the house that I caught sight of him. He was standing in the lounge watching the television, which our dear son Philip had left on.

Lydia Skinner

SK: Aagh!

Hear-Hear!

My daughters, Sarah and Becki, then aged about four and two, had two pet snails and were playing 'Snail Races' in the garden. 'Ready, steady, go,' shouted Becki to the snails. After a slight pause – and obviously disappointing results – Sarah said: 'Becki, your snail's deaf. He didn't hear you say, "Go".'

Jenni Beddington

TERRIBLE PETS

What's your problem!

One Saturday evening I was happily absorbed in a book when the sound of a sheep bleating appeared closer and louder than usual. On looking out into the garden I saw that one of the sheep had jumped the field fence and was in the actual 'run', panicking that she couldn't get back to her 'pals'.

I went out into the garden and began running parallel to the run to encourage her to return to the field. On seeing me, she panicked all the more and hared off down the run, bleating at full volume. Nothing for it, I thought, so donning a pair of green wellies and grabbing a walking stick I duly clambered over my fence (4 ft) and endeavoured to shoo her back while attempting, semaphore-fashion, to attract the attention of the farmer. I had no idea sheep could jump so high, but, like a steeplechaser, she vaulted over the connecting fences in the run. Then, realizing she could not get back into the field that way, she turned around and headed back towards me at a rate of knots hitting me squarely in the lower regions of my body. Up – and over her – I went, landing flat on my face in a clump of nettles but still clutching my stick. It was only then that I realized that she would get to a dead-end, and be forced to turn around and head back again. Not wanting to be trampled over – and receive hoof-marks all over my back and head – I managed to jump up (I'm just out of my early forties) only to see her heading straight for me once again

Where to go, I wondered? Two choices – the nettles again or the barbed-wire field fence. By this time my adversary had decided not to tangle with this person, clutching a stick, and had pushed herself through my fence and into my garden. Gotcha I thought. But now I had to surmount the four-foot garden fence again, complete with stick. By this time the pain had reached my brain, but the sight of this manic sheep charging around my garden spurred me on. With considerable effort, I clambered over the fence suffering still more damage to lower portions of my body – thighs this time! Once over, and brandishing my stick at head height, I proceeded to chase the sheep

62

through the flower-beds, bobbing her with my stick whenever I got close enough and muttering 'Come here you, little bugger'. My neighbours' dog, spying the stick moving backwards and forwards, decided to join in, chasing along her side of the fence and barking furiously.

Fortunately, the end was in sight. My adversary decided to return to the run, through my fence, and head once more for her 'pals'. I continued to pursue 'her', climbing my fence yet again only to see that, seemingly totally unaware of the chaos she had caused, she had finally managed to clamber back into the field and was calmly chewing grass with the rest of the flock.

By this time, I was in a state of complete collapse, but I still had to clamber back over the fence and get indoors without injuring myself further. Needless to say, it was not until I slid (gently) into the bath that I could see the funny side.

Ms Margaret Green

Left, right, left right

In the garden we keep an old washing-up bowl under which we keep a tin of food for feeding the cat in the morning.

One morning, about 2 a.m., we were woken by a strange scraping noise, and thought it was probably roaming cats trying to get at the food under the bowl. We tried to return to sleep but the strange noise persisted and, eventually overcome by curiosity, we went to see what was happening. On opening the back door, the bowl, to our utter astonishment, was trotting down the garden path at a fair rate of knots. Not being the sort who enjoys unpleasant surprises I told my husband to see what was happening. Very slowly he lifted the bowl and there, underneath, was one of the biggest hedgehogs I have ever seen with a tin of cat food stuck on his head!

We took the tin off and let him go, which he did very rapidly. Now, we put him his own saucer of food out at night, but we will never forget the sight of that bowl trotting off down the garden path.

Mrs Joan Hodskinson

THE END!

CARY 95.